# HISTORY & GEOGRAPHY 402
# SEAPORT CITIES

**Author:**
Theresa K. Buskey, B.A., J.D.

**Editor:**
Alan Christopherson, M.S.

**Assistant Editor:**
Annette M. Walker, B.S.

**Media Credits:**
**Page 3:** © Ron Chapple Studios, Thinkstock; **4:** © Josef Hanus, iStock, Thinkstock; **7:** © Georgios Kollidas, iStock, Thinkstock; **11:** © Greg Ward, Hemera, Thinkstock; **13:** © KJA, iStock, Thinkstock; **15:** © CBCK Christine, iStock, Thinkstock; **16:** © JRabski, iStock, Thinkstock; **18:** © shells1, iStock, Thinkstock; **23:** © Jess Yu, iStock, Thinkstock; **26:** © rigamondis, iStock, Thinkstock; **28:** © ronniechua, iStock, Thinkstock; **30:** © Jupiterimages, Photos.com, Thinkstock; **31:** © Yali Shi, iStock, Thinkstock; **33:** © Dong Haojun, iStock, Thinkstock; **38:** © raufmiski, iStock, Thinkstock; **40:** © Dorling Kindersley, Thinkstock; **43:** © Amanda Lewis, iStock, Thinkstock; **45:** © takepicsforfun, iStock, Thinkstock; **47:** (left) © rez-art, iStock, Thinkstock; (right) © Toru Uchida, iStock, Thinkstock; **48:** © ManuKro, iStock, Thinkstock; **53:** krzych 34, iStock, Thinkstock; **55:** Baloncici, iStock, Thinkstock; **57:** starekase, iStock, Thinkstock; **62:** © Jupiterimages, Photos.com, Thinkstock; **64:** © John Helgason, iStock, Thinkstock; **66:** © deyangeorgiev, iStock, Thinkstock.

All maps in this book © Image Resources, unless otherwise stated.

**Alpha Omega**
PUBLICATIONS

**804 N. 2nd Ave. E.**
**Rock Rapids, IA 51246-1759**

LIFEPAC®

# HISTORY & GEOGRAPHY

## STUDENT BOOK

▶ **4th Grade** | Unit 2

Alpha Omega
PUBLICATIONS

# SEAPORT CITIES

Have you ever taken a trip on an ocean liner? In this **LIFEPAC®** you are going to follow the cruise of an ocean liner that will visit four famous seaport cities: Sydney in Australia, Hong Kong on the coast of China, Istanbul in Turkey, and London in Great Britain. You will learn about the geography, history, and life of these exciting cities. You will start and finish in San Francisco in the United States.

## Objectives

**Read these objectives.** The objectives tell you what you will be able to do when you have successfully completed this LIFEPAC. Each section will list according to the numbers below what objectives will be met in that section. When you have finished this LIFEPAC, you should be able to:

1. Locate on a world map the places mentioned in the text and places along the route.
2. Tell about the history of each of the seaport cities.
3. Name the places in each city that are of special interest to visitors.
4. Tell a little about how people live in each city.
5. Recognize geography terms and use them.

# 1. SYDNEY, THE GREATEST DOWN-UNDER SEAPORT

Take the world map out of the center of the LIFEPAC. Label the continents, the equator, and the major oceans. Look at a globe or world map any time you need help finding something.

Your cruise begins in the port of San Francisco. The harbor is one of the world's largest, covering 450 square miles. The city itself is built on a peninsula between the Pacific Ocean and San Francisco Bay. Early European explorers had trouble finding the mouth of the bay because it is so often very foggy. Today the Golden Gate Bridge spans the harbor mouth. Your journey begins by sailing under it.

The ship sails out of San Francisco Bay southwestward across the Pacific Ocean. South of the equator, in southern Australia, lies another magnificent harbor. As the ship passes beneath Harbour Bridge (note the British spelling), memories of San Francisco's Golden Gate remain. However, no trace of fog hides this city. The harbor is part of Sydney, the largest city in Australia and the greatest seaport "down under" the equator.

Put a mark on your world map for the cities of San Francisco and Sydney. Label them. Draw on the map the ship's route from San Francisco to Sydney.

# Objectives

**Review these objectives.** When you have completed this section, you should be able to:

1. Locate on a world map the places mentioned in the text and places along the route.
2. Tell about the history of each of the seaport cities.
3. Name the places in each city that are of special interest to visitors.
4. Tell a little about how people live in each city.
5. Recognize geography terms and use them.

# Vocabulary

**Study these new words.** Learning the meanings of these words is a good study habit and will improve your understanding of this LIFEPAC.

**ancestors** (an' ses tər). Parents, grandparents, great-grandparents, and so on, back to Adam and Eve; the people from whom one is descended.

**ballast** (bal' əst). Something heavy, carried in a ship to steady it.

**expedition** (ek spə dish' ən). A journey with a special purpose.

**ferry** (fer' ē). A boat to carry people a short distance.

**landmark** (land' märk). Something easily seen; used as a guide.

**penal colony** (pē' nəl kol' ə nē). A settlement made in another country where lawbreakers are sent for punishment.

**port** (pôrt). A harbor; a place where ships can load and unload; city or town by a harbor.

**Portuguese man-of-war** (pôr' chə gēz' man uv wôr). A jellyfish-like sea animal that has stinging tentacles.

**volunteer** (vol' ən tir'). A person who offers to work or help without pay.

**Note:** *All vocabulary words in this LIFEPAC appear in* **boldface** *print the first time they are used. If you are unsure of the meaning when you are reading, study the definitions given.*

**Pronunciation Key:** hat, āge, cãre, fär; let, ēqual, tėrm; it, īce; hot, ōpen, ôrder; oil; out; cup, put, rüle; child; long; thin; /ŦH/ for then; /zh/ for measure; /u/ or /ə/ represents /a/ in about, /e/ in taken, /i/ in pencil, /o/ in lemon, and /u/ in circus.

**Complete these map activities.**

**1.1** Draw in and label the Golden Gate Bridge.

**1.2** Put a "**B**" on San Francisco Bay.

**1.3** Circle the peninsula San Francisco is on.

**1.4** Put an "**X**" on the mouth of the Sacramento River.

**1.5** San Francisco is (what direction?) _____ of Oakland.

**1.6** Because it is a deep bay used to shelter ships, San Francisco Bay is also a

_____ .

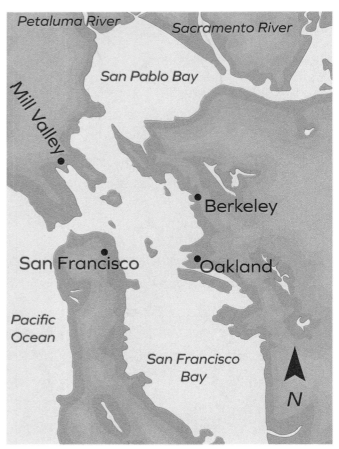

| San Francisco Bay Area

**Teacher check:**

Initials _____     Date _____

# Penal Colony

The first European to report on Australia was a famous British explorer, Captain James Cook. Cook, a navy officer, was sent on a scientific **expedition** to the South Pacific in 1768. He sailed southwest from England across the Atlantic Ocean and around the bottom of South America. Sailing around the world, he stopped along the east coast of Australia on his way home in 1770.

There he sailed into a large bay surrounded by a green land of trees and flowers. The land reminded him so much of his home that he named it New South Wales. He claimed it all for England and named the bay Botany Bay. On his way north, he passed another bay which he named Port Jackson but did not explore it.

| Captain James Cook

Britain at that time needed a place to send criminals from its badly crowded prisons. It was decided to start a **penal colony** in Australia. The first group of prisoners, called the First Fleet, landed in 1788. They were supposed to go to Botany Bay, but the fleet commander, Captain Arthur Phillip, decided Port Jackson was a better spot. The huge harbor was the site chosen for the colony's first settlement, named Sydney, after a British government official.

The First Fleet included about 300 soldiers and their families, 550 male prisoners, and 200 female prisoners. The prisoners were to serve their jail time working in the new colony. After their term ended, they were free and could be given land to start a new life. Very few had any chance of getting enough money to pay for a return trip to England, so being sent to Australia really meant never going home again.

The first years were very difficult for the settlers. The prisoners were forced to work and were beaten for any wrongdoing. Most of the criminals were city dwellers who did not know how to farm or build. The farm animals ran away. Many of their crops did not grow, and the supply ships came late. The people almost starved to death.

The British government continued to send criminals to New South Wales until 1848. In all, about 83,000 prisoners were "transported" to serve their prison terms in the area. By that time, the colony's farms were doing well, many British people were coming "down under" to live, and Sydney was a growing city.

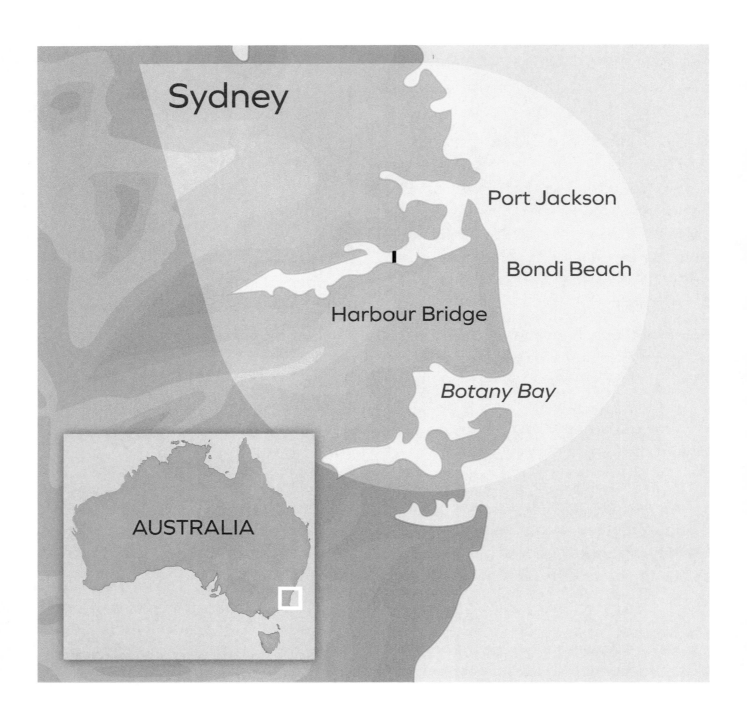

**Complete these sentences.**

**1.7** Britain decided to make Australia a _____ .

**1.8** The first group of prisoners sent to Sydney were called the _____

_____ .

**1.9** The man who first reported about Australia in Europe was _____

_____ .

**1.10** Sydney was founded on the harbor of _____ .

**Answer these questions using complete sentences.**

**1.11** Why were the first years difficult for the new Australians?

_____

_____

_____

**1.12** What name did Captain Cook give to eastern Australia? Why?

_____

_____

_____

**1.13** Why did the criminals stay in Sydney after they had served their sentences?

_____

_____

_____

Sydney became a successful colony because of sheep. An Australian farmer grew a type of sheep that did well on the grasslands and produced very thick, fine wool. This created a large ranching and wool industry. It attracted free settlers, merchants, bankers, and others. By 1842 Sydney had grown to the point that it elected a city government.

The city grew steadily. In 1851 gold was discovered in New South Wales. That set off a gold rush, as men flooded into the area to try to become rich. Many of the people stayed even after gold was found in other parts of Australia.

The different colonies on the continent of Australia joined together in 1901 to create the Commonwealth of Australia. Sydney became the capital of the state of New South Wales. Over the years, Australia slowly became independent from Britain. The Australians did not fight a war for independence, as the United States did. Australia is part of the British Commonwealth of Nations, countries that were once British colonies. The Queen of England still is the ruler of all Commonwealth countries, but she and the British government have no power over them at all.

---

 **Complete these sentences.**

**1.14** _____ was discovered in 1851 in New South Wales.

**1.15** Sydney became a successful colony because of _____ .

**1.16** Sydney started a city government in _____ .

**1.17** In 1901 the colonies in Australia joined together to form the

_____ .

# City of Sydney

Sydney is located in Port Jackson, also called Sydney Harbour (British spelling again). The harbor is one of the world's finest. There are 150 miles of **coast** inside Port Jackson, and it covers 21 square miles. Thousands of boats dock in the many bays and coves around Sydney. The harbor handles millions of tons of cargo each year on thousands of ships. Coal, meat, wheat, and wool are the main exports shipped out of Sydney.

| Flag of Australia

Officially the city of Sydney covers only about 15 square miles right near where the First Fleet landed. However, if you think of all the city area around Port Jackson as the Sydney area, it covers about 5,000 square miles and has over four million people. It is the largest city in Australia and the busiest port in the Southern Hemisphere.

Very little planning went into the building of the city of Sydney. The early governors were too busy trying to control the criminals and stay alive to plan a beautiful city. But slowly, nicer public and private buildings were built. Large, pretty houses were built as people made money from sheep ranching, farming, trading, and gold mining.

Iron was brought to Sydney as **ballast** to add weight to nearly empty ships. The iron was left behind so the ships could carry more on their return trip. The iron was melted down and used to create beautiful decorated railings and balconies for the newly-built houses. This iron-work is called "Sydney lace." There are many different styles and types. It decorates many houses in the older areas of Sydney.

| Sydney Lace

**Decorate these hillside house fronts.**

**1.18** Make "Sydney lace" railings. Color them in light colors.

**Teacher check:**

Initials _____ Date _____

Sydney has two **landmarks** that are easy to recognize. The first is the Sydney Harbour Bridge. It links the downtown area with the north side of the harbor. It was finished in 1932. It is a metal bridge with a high arch that runs above the road. It is nicknamed "the coat hanger" by the people of Sydney.

There is a funny story about the ceremony when the bridge was opened in 1932. The head of the government of Australia, the Prime Minister, was supposed to cut a ribbon in front of the bridge to officially open it. Just as he was about to do it, a soldier who did not like the Prime Minister rode up on a horse and cut the ribbon with his sword! They had to tie the ribbon together and cut it again!

Before the bridge was opened, people had to cross the harbor on ferries. Dozens of **ferries** carried people back and forth across the harbor in the 1920s. By 1928 they were carrying about 46 million people across the harbor each year. After the bridge was built, people began riding the train or driving across the harbor. Only a few ferries still cross the harbor today.

The most famous landmark in Sydney is the Opera House. It is built right on the harbor near the landing spot of the First Fleet. The roof of the Opera House is covered with tall, white, arched roofs that look like sails in the wind. The Opera House has four main auditoriums and took fourteen years to build. It was opened in 1973 by Queen Elizabeth II of England. Today, it is the home of the Sydney Symphony Orchestra, the Australian Opera, and other famous performing groups.

| The Sydney Opera House and the Sydney Harbour Bridge

**Complete the following.**

**1.19** Name the two major landmarks in Sydney.

a. _____

b. _____

**1.20** The harbor of Port Jackson covers _____ square miles.

**1.21** The Harbour Bridge is nicknamed the _____ .

**1.22** The decorative iron railings are called _____ .

**Answer _true_ or _false_.**

**1.23** _____ The city of Sydney was not carefully planned.

**1.24** _____ Before the bridge was opened people had to cross the harbor on a ferry.

**1.25** _____ The Opera House was opened in 1955 by the Prime Minister.

**1.26** _____ Coal, meat, wheat, and wool are the main exports from Sydney.

# Sydneysiders

Sydney is a city that is very spread out. Very few people live in apartments, because everyone wants to have his own home on a piece of land. That is very important to Australians, so the city spreads out in every direction. There are tall buildings downtown for the businesses, but the people live away from downtown in their own houses.

Sydney is in the Southern Hemisphere. That means the seasons are the opposite of what we have in the Northern Hemisphere. Sydney has winter in June, July, and August. It has summer in December, January, and February. Christmas comes at the hottest time of the year.

It is very warm in Sydney all year around because it is located just south of the Tropic of Capricorn. The temperature is usually in the high 70s in the summer (January) and in the 50s in the winter (July).

Because it is so warm and sunny, the people of Sydney, called Sydneysiders, like to be outdoors. Sydney has lovely beaches where people go to swim and sunbathe. Bondi Beach is the most famous and can be very crowded on holidays.

| Bondi Beach

The beaches are guarded by **volunteer** life-saving clubs. These clubs each have their own color uniforms and caps so people can find them in the crowds. They practice so they can rescue people who start to drown in the ocean. They hold contests where they race other clubs in lifeboats and swimming.

Long nets are spread across the water away from the beaches. These nets are to keep sharks away from the beach. There are many sharks in the ocean near Sydney. A sharp lookout is kept for them along the beaches, and a bell is rung when one is spotted. As scary as sharks are, very few people are hurt by them. More people are hurt by the **Portuguese man-of-war**. These jellyfish-like sea animals do not kill, but they have a very painful sting.

| Portuguese man-of-war

Sydneysiders also like to go "bushwalking." Australians call all places outside of a town or city "the bush." Sydney has several large national parks close to the city. People form clubs that go bushwalking together on weekends in these parks.

**Match these items.**

| 1.27 | _____ | Portuguese man-of-war | a. | winter |
| 1.28 | _____ | bushwalking | b. | painful sting |
| 1.29 | _____ | Bondi | c. | hiking outside the city |
| 1.30 | _____ | July | d. | summer |
| 1.31 | _____ | January | e. | Beach |

**Answer *true* or *false*.**

**1.32** _____ The bush in Australia is the area of very dense trees around streams.

**1.33** _____ Nets are set up along the beaches to keep sharks away.

**1.34** _____ Beach lifeguards are well-paid in Sydney.

**1.35** _____ Sydney gets very cold in the winter.

**1.36** _____ Sydney is a very spread-out city.

 **Choose one of these Australian animals.**

**1.37** Look up information on it and write a paragraph about the animal. Draw a picture, make a puppet, or make a mask of it.

| | | |
|---|---|---|
| dingo | wombat | kangaroo |
| lyre bird | wallaby | duck-billed platypus |

**Teacher check:**

Initials _____ Date _____

Yacht racing is very popular with Sydneysiders. Yachts are boats of all sizes and kinds. Races for the different types are always being held in the harbor. The most famous race is the Sydney-Hobart Yacht Race. It is a race from Sydney Harbour to Hobart, on the **island** of Tasmania 630 miles to the south. The race begins in Sydney on December the 26th and may take a couple of weeks to finish if the weather is bad.

The biggest event in Sydney is the Royal Easter Show. It is like a giant state fair held at Easter time each year. It began as a show for farm animals and crops. It grew to include a huge carnival. There are performers, a rodeo, balloon rides, and lots of food.

You can tell that Sydney was founded by people from Britain. The cars drive on the left side of the road, just like in England. Soccer, rugby (an English game similar to football), and cricket (an English game similar to baseball) are all popular in Sydney. So is the English passion for drinking tea.

Sydneysiders are not ashamed of the fact that many of their **ancestors** were criminals. In fact, they are proud of how they overcame their past to build a new nation in the Southern Hemisphere. Many of the criminals became good citizens after serving their sentences. A few even became rich and built some of the beautiful homes around Sydney Harbour. A Sydneysider is proud of any "transported" criminal in his family tree. It shows him to be a real Australian.

| Yacht racing

**Answer *true* or *false*.**

**1.38** _____ The Sydney-Hobart Yacht Race ends in Tasmania.

**1.39** _____ The Royal Easter Show is like a large state fair.

**1.40** _____ Sydneysiders are ashamed of any transported criminals in their family tree.

**1.41** _____ Yachts are a special type of boat that is always the same size and type.

**Complete the following.**

**1.42** Name three things that show how Sydney was founded by British people.

a. _____

b. _____

c. _____

**Draw the Australian flag.**

**1.43** Find the picture of the flag in this LIFEPAC. Using a sheet of white paper and crayons, color your flag.

> **Teacher check:**
>
> Initials _____ Date _____

**Review the material in this section to prepare for the Self Test.** The Self Test will check your understanding of this section. Any items you miss on this test will show you what areas you will need to restudy in order to prepare for the unit test.

# SELF TEST 1

**Review from LIFEPAC 401. Choose the correct letter on the map for each word listed in activities 1.01 - 1.010** (2 points each answer). Some will be used more than once.

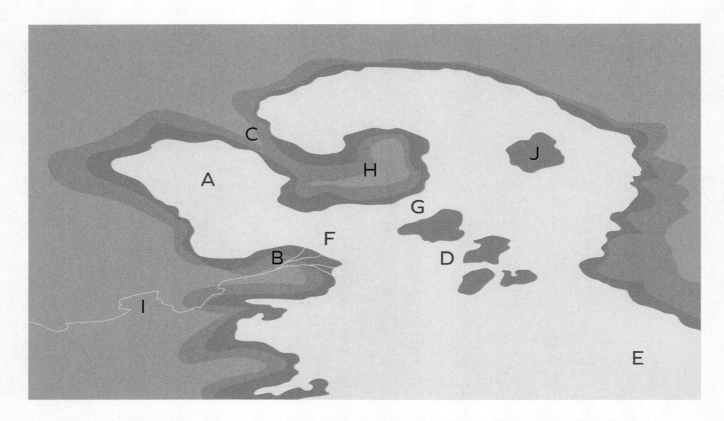

| | | | | |
|---|---|---|---|---|
| **1.01** | _____ island | **1.02** | _____ isthmus |
| **1.03** | _____ strait | **1.04** | _____ delta |
| **1.05** | _____ mouth | **1.06** | _____ bay |
| **1.07** | _____ gulf | **1.08** | _____ archipelago |
| **1.09** | _____ peninsula | **1.010** | _____ river |

**Match each answer with the correct letter** (3 points each answer).

| | | |
|---|---|---|
| **1.011** | _____ Captain James Cook | a.  decoration made of iron |
| **1.012** | _____ Port Jackson | b.  first explorer to Australia |
| **1.013** | _____ Sydney Lace | c.  nation formed by the colonies |
| **1.014** | _____ Opera House | d.  like a large state fair |
| **1.015** | _____ Sydneysiders | e.  crosses Sydney's harbor |
| **1.016** | _____ Sydney Harbour Bridge | f.  state where Sydney is capital |
| **1.017** | _____ New South Wales | g.  people who live in Sydney |
| **1.018** | _____ First Fleet | h.  Sydney's harbor |
| **1.019** | _____ Commonwealth of Australia | i.  first transported prisoners |
| | | j.  landmark with sail-like roof |
| **1.020** | _____ Royal Easter Show | |

**Answer *true* or *false*** (2 points each answer).

**1.021** _____ The first British colonists in Sydney almost starved.

**1.022** _____ Sydney is a very spread-out city.

**1.023** _____ Sydney is Australia's largest city.

**1.024** _____ Sydney Harbor is the busiest port south of the equator.

**1.025** _____ The lifeguards on Sydney's beaches are volunteers.

**1.026** _____ The Atlantic Ocean is between San Francisco and Sydney.

**1.027** _____ San Francisco is "down under."

**1.028** _____ The Golden Gate Bridge crosses the mouth of San Francisco Bay.

**Write the correct answer** (4 points each answer).

**1.029** Why did the prisoners stay in Australia after they were freed?

_____

_____

**1.030**   How do Sydney's seasons differ from ours? Why?

_____

_____

_____

**1.031**   Name two outdoor activities the people of Sydney enjoy (2 points each answer).

a. _____

b. _____

**1.032**   How did Australia become independent from Great Britain?

_____

_____

_____

**Put the correct answer on the blank** (3 points each answer).

**1.033**   The colony of Sydney was started as a _____ colony.

**1.034**   San Francisco is built on a _____ between the Pacific Ocean and the Bay.

**1.035**   Sydney became successful when people started raising _____ .

**1.036**   Men rushed to move to Sydney in 1851 because _____ was discovered nearby.

**1.037**   Before the bridge was built, people used to cross the harbor on a

_____ .

**1.038**   The beaches near Sydney are protected by _____ to keep the sharks away.

# 2. HONG KONG, MARKETPLACE OF ASIA

The ship leaves Sydney's harbor and sails north past great coral reefs. From the Coral Sea, the ship will continue past groups of Pacific islands. For days it will continue northwest, until the archipelago of the Philippine Islands is left behind to the south. One evening, a fairyland of moving and twinkling lights comes into view. They rise right out of the South China Sea and sparkle like jewels in a crown. The ship is approaching Hong Kong, a great trading center in China.

## Objectives

**Review these objectives.** When you have completed this section, you should be able to:

1. Locate on a world map the places mentioned in the text and places along the route.
2. Tell about the history of each of the seaport cities.
3. Name the places in each city that are of special interest to visitors.
4. Tell a little about how people live in each city.
5. Recognize geography terms and use them.

## Vocabulary

**Study these new words.** Learning the meanings of these words is a good study habit and will improve your understanding of this LIFEPAC.

**addictive** (ə dik′ tiv). Causing a person to become a slave to a habit.

**manufacture** (man′ yə fak′ chər). To make a product, especially by machine, and in large amounts.

**pollute** (pə lüt′). To make dirty or impure.

**refugee** (ref′ yü jē). A person who flees for safety from danger.

**Pronunciation Key:** hat, āge, cãre, fär; let, ēqual, tėrm; it, īce; hot, ōpen, ôrder; oil; out; cup, put, rüle; child; long; thin; /ŦH/ for then; /zh/ for measure; /u/ or /ə/ represents /a/ in about, /e/ in taken, /i/ in pencil, /o/ in lemon, and /u/ in circus.

# The Taking of Hong Kong

Britain used to own many other countries, called colonies, all over the world (including the United States). Hong Kong became a British colony in the 1800s. The British took the land after defeating the Chinese in two wars. They were called the Opium Wars, and the British treated the Chinese very badly in those wars.

Britain wanted to trade goods with China for its tea and silk, but the Chinese did not want to trade goods; they wanted to make payment in gold or silver for their merchandise. The British did not like paying this way.

The British began trading opium for Chinese goods rather than paying in gold. Opium is a drug that is **addictive**. People who take it feel good for a little while and then must have more of the drug. It ruins people's lives, because they do not want anything except more opium. The British knew this, but they made a great deal of money trading opium for valuable Chinese goods.

The Opium Wars were fought when the Chinese tried to stop the opium trade that was hurting their people. The British used their stronger army to force the trade to continue. They took Hong Kong, with its huge harbor, to use as a base for the trade.

The British forced China to give them Hong Kong Island in 1841. The Chinese gave them the peninsula across from the island, Kowloon, in 1860. In 1898 the British leased, or rented, the New Territories north of Kowloon and many nearby islands for 99 years. These three areas are the colony of Hong Kong.

---

 **Complete this map activity.**

**2.1** On your world map, label the Coral Sea, the Philippine Islands, and the South China Sea. Mark and label Hong Kong. Draw the ship's route from Sydney to Hong Kong. (If you need more space, write where you find room and draw arrows to those items.)

**Teacher check:**

Initials _____     Date _____

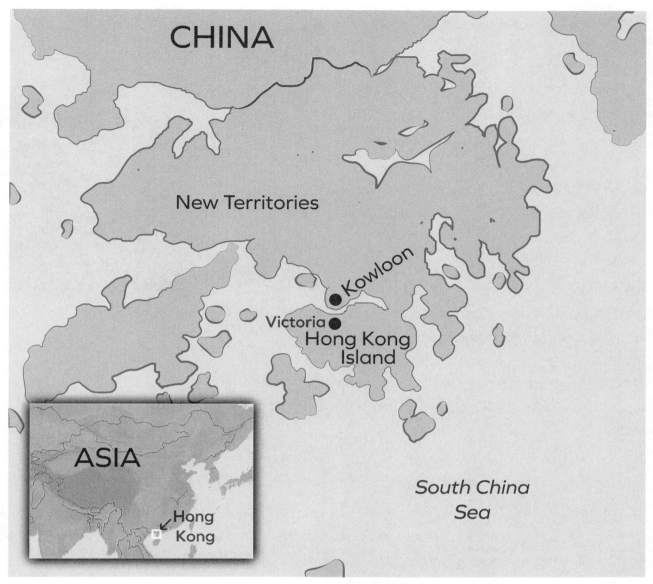

| Hong Kong

**Put the correct answer on the blank.**

2.2     The British defeated the Chinese in the _____ Wars.

2.3     Hong Kong was a colony owned by _____ .

2.4     The British forced the Chinese to trade _____
        for tea and silk.

2.5     The three parts of Hong Kong are _____ ,

        _____ , and _____ .

The port of Hong Kong became a busy, wealthy place due to the trade with China. Many Chinese people came there to find jobs. Opium continued to be a major trade item until the early 1900s.

During World War II, Hong Kong was a dangerous place. The city was bombed and then taken over by Japanese soldiers. One of every three people left the city or died. After the war ended, the people returned and rebuilt the city.

In 1949 a communist government was set up in China, and many Chinese left their country. A flood of **refugees** swarmed into

| Refugee villages

Hong Kong. The city became unbelievably crowded. The colony allowed them to stay and built huge apartments with tiny rooms for them to live in. A new apartment building was started every ten days. Hong Kong is now one of the most crowded cities in the world!

Some of these refugees were wealthy people who knew the communists would take everything away from them. They started new businesses in Hong Kong with the money they brought with them.

The refugees who were poor came with only a willingness to work. They had lost everything and would work hard for very little money. Hong Kong became a place where things could be **manufactured** very quickly and cheaply. The government allowed the businesses to work however they wanted and kept the taxes very low. As a result, Hong Kong became a busy, hard-working city with many businesses. Today, the people of Hong Kong are known for their hard work and for always trying to make more money.

China wanted Hong Kong back, but Britain refused because it knew the communist government would ruin the city. But the communists became more interested in making money in the 1980s, and the 99-year lease of the New Territories was going to run out in 1997. In 1984 Britain agreed that the colony would all become a part of China again in 1997. China agreed to not change Hong Kong's way of working for fifty years.

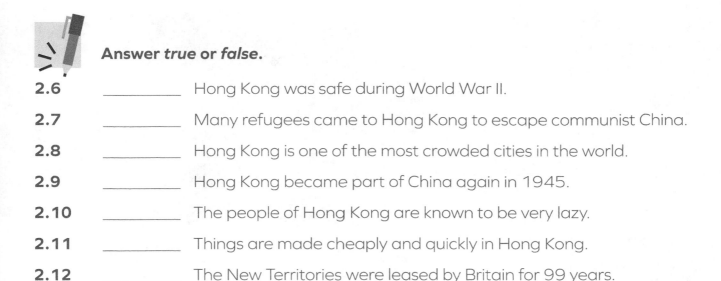

**Answer *true* or *false*.**

**2.6** _____ Hong Kong was safe during World War II.

**2.7** _____ Many refugees came to Hong Kong to escape communist China.

**2.8** _____ Hong Kong is one of the most crowded cities in the world.

**2.9** _____ Hong Kong became part of China again in 1945.

**2.10** _____ The people of Hong Kong are known to be very lazy.

**2.11** _____ Things are made cheaply and quickly in Hong Kong.

**2.12** _____ The New Territories were leased by Britain for 99 years.

# Hong Kong Today

Hong Kong means "fragrant harbor." That magnificent harbor covers 17 square miles. A whole fleet of ships can come in at one time. When ships were powered by sails, it was important that the harbor be open in two directions, so the ships could sail no matter which way the wind was blowing.

| Flag of Hong Kong

The former colonial capital of Hong Kong is the city of Victoria on Hong Kong Island. The island is connected to Kowloon by a subway tunnel, a road tunnel, and many ferries. If you are in a big hurry, you can go across by helicopter! Hong Kong no longer has a capital city since it is a special administrative region in China.

Almost six million people live in Hong Kong. Most of those people have to live in the cities of Kowloon or Victoria. That is because land on the island of Hong Kong and Kowloon is covered with mountains. There is very little space where buildings can be put, and it is all very expensive. Much of the land in the New Territories is needed for farms. Thus, only the twenty square miles inside the cities are available for homes. That would be like taking all of the people in the state of Indiana and putting them into the city of Newark, New Jersey!

The people of Hong Kong work to create new land to build on. The runway of the main airport extends out into the harbor. Dirt and rocks were brought in to build it there. More land is always being built in the ocean this way. Houses and apartments are built on the sides of mountains after digging out a place to put

| Victoria Harbor, Hong Kong

them. Old buildings are constantly being torn down to build bigger new ones. Buildings are very tall so that a small piece of land can be used to make a large amount of living space. It is very different from spread-out Sydney!

Many people in Hong Kong do not try to find homes on land. They live in boats that float in the harbor. The boat homes have a cover over part of the deck. They are called *sampans*. There are schools, shops, and doctors on boats to serve them. These people used to make their living by fishing, but the water around Hong Kong is too **polluted** now. There are not many fish anymore, so most of the boat people work in factories or do odd jobs to earn money.

Most of the people of Hong Kong are Chinese. Until 1997, however, the British ran the government. The fair British laws made people trust the government. That trust allowed people to go to Hong Kong and build businesses there.

Beautiful things are made in Hong Kong's many factories and art shops. Shoes, clothes, furniture, carvings, and jade jewelry are made and sold. Hong Kong tailors will make clothes by copying from a picture. The customer chooses the cloth and in one day has a new outfit made just for him.

Hong Kong is a duty-free port. This means that the government does not charge any taxes on goods that are brought in from other countries. Many people visit Hong Kong just so they can go shopping there. The prices are low because goods are all duty-free. The same things might cost quite a bit more in the United States because of the taxes paid to bring it into the country.

 **Match the following.**

**2.13** _____ Hong Kong

**2.14** _____ duty-free

**2.15** _____ sampan

**2.16** _____ New Territories

**2.17** _____ Victoria

a. needed for farmland

b. boat home

c. "fragrant harbor"

d. former capital of the colony

e. no taxes for goods coming into the country

 **Put the correct answer on the blank.**

**2.18** The water around Hong Kong is too _____ for people to make a living by fishing.

**2.19** Until 1997 the _____ ran the government of Hong Kong.

**2.20** List some ways people in Hong Kong find room to build and live.

a. _____

b. _____

c. _____

d. _____

# Chinese Life

The people of Hong Kong are famous for their hard work. Many of the people were refugees who know what it is like to be starving. They are afraid to have that happen again and work hard to prevent it. Very few people in Hong Kong are Christians. They do not know how to trust God for their needs. They only know how to work and get more money.

People work long hours in the factories, then often get part-time jobs at night. Shopkeepers have their stores open sixteen hours a day, seven days a week. Children often work with their parents at home, assembling parts or packing goods to be shipped to other countries. Most people want to save enough money to start their own business. Thousands of small shops in Hong Kong sell food, clothes, jewelry, shoes, and every other thing that can be bought or sold. That is another reason so many people like to go shopping there.

The people of Hong Kong are also famous for their food, and visitors come for that as well. Housewives in Hong Kong insist on fresh food. They go to the market every day to buy their groceries, but these groceries are not like your nearby supermarket. The chicken or pig is alive until the cook buys it! Vegetables and fruit are freshly picked. The farmers in the New Territories grow eight crops a year to keep up with the demand for fresh food. Communist China also makes a great deal of money selling fresh food to Hong Kong.

| Hong Kong restaurant

The restaurants in Hong Kong are famous all over the world. No one knows how many there are in the city. Hundreds of small businesses sell meals in little rooms and on street corners, but there are also huge, elegant places that are very expensive. There you can get shark fin or bird's nest soup. You can also get Peking duck, which has been cooked for a whole day. The choices are endless. The people of Hong Kong love to eat out and expect to have many good choices.

The people of Hong Kong enjoy sports. They especially like soccer and cricket, but both of those games require large fields to play, and open land is hard to find in Hong Kong. Basketball has become popular because it can be played on small city courts or even on top of buildings.

In Hong Kong you can see a type of entertainment called Chinese opera. It is very beautiful. The actors dress in bright costumes and vivid makeup. The costumes are decorated with gold thread and feathers. The operas tell ancient Chinese stories using music and carefully planned movements of the hands. It is fun to watch even if you do not understand the words.

Chinese people love to gamble, and that is true in Hong Kong as well. A favorite game is mah-jong, which is similar to poker, but is played with small domino-shaped blocks instead of cards. The Royal Jockey Club racetrack raises money for worthy causes by giving away most of the gambling money spent at the horse races. The Chinese do not give to people in need, outside of their family, in the way Americans do; but they will gamble to help others.

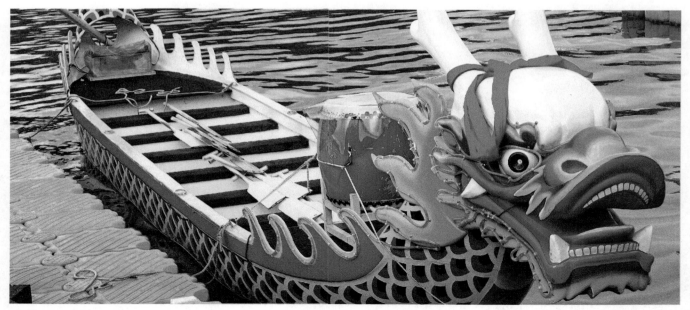

| Dragon boats

Several important festivals are celebrated in Hong Kong during the year. Often these are based on the Chinese religion which believes in many false gods and spirits. The most important festival is the Chinese New Year in late January or early February. This is the most important celebration in the Chinese **culture**. Everything is scrubbed clean, people get new clothes, everyone eats all they can, and gifts of money are exchanged. In mid-June there is a Dragon Boat Festival. Beautifully decorated Dragon Boats race each other in the harbor. Another festival honors the Chinese goddess of the sea with a parade of decorated boats. Even though few people in Hong Kong are farmers, there is a harvest festival in the fall, also.

The island of Cheung Chau in Hong Kong also celebrates the Bun Festival in the Spring. A four-day holiday is held for the ghosts of people killed by pirates that used to live on the island. The festival is to make them happy. Tall towers of buns are set out to feed the ghosts. Since there aren't really any ghosts, real people take the buns to eat. The buns are considered lucky. The ones higher up on the tower are the luckiest, so the young men race each other to the top to get the highest buns.

**Put the correct answer on the blank.**

**2.21**    The people of Hong Kong are famous for their _____ and their

_____ .

**2.22**    The most important celebration in the Chinese culture is the _____

_____ .

**2.23**    In the Spring, the island of Cheung Chau celebrates the _____

_____ to make ghosts happy.

**2.24**    A favorite gambling game is _____ , which uses small blocks like dominoes.

**2.25**    Cooks insist that the food they buy is _____ .

**2.26**    _____ tells ancient Chinese stories using beautiful costumes, music, and hand movements.

**2.27**    People come to Hong Kong for the _____ and the _____ .

**2.28**    It is hard to play soccer and cricket because both require _____

_____ .

**2.29**    Farmers in the New Territories grow _____ crops a year.

The Chinese religion is very different from Christianity. It is a mixture of many religions. Confucianism is a belief in the importance of good behavior. Confucius taught people to honor their parents, tell the truth, and work hard. Confucius was the most important person in Chinese history. Most Chinese people try to follow his teachings. But Chinese people also believe in Taoism (dou' iz əm), which teaches that there are many small gods that protect the sea, travelers, kitchens, and everything else. Buddhism is also part of Chinese religion. It came from India and teaches that when you die you are born again as another person on earth. The people of Hong Kong believe <u>all</u> of these teachings and more.

| Statue of Confucius

Most important of all, the Chinese people believe in good and bad luck. They always consult a *feng shui* man, or fortune teller, before they do anything important. This person tells them exactly what to do to have good luck. They may have to make an offering to the gods, wear a certain color, or even rearrange the furniture in their apartment! The Bible tells us not to listen to fortune tellers because they do not speak from God. The people of Hong Kong spend much money and time trying to find and keep good luck. Jesus teaches us that we need salvation and to trust Him to direct our lives.

**Put the correct answer on the blank.**

**2.30**   List the three religions that are a part of Chinese beliefs.

a. _____

b. _____

c. _____

**2.31**   The people of Hong Kong always ask the advice of a _____
before making any important decision.

**2.32**   The most important man in Chinese history was _____ .

**2.33**   The people of Hong Kong spend a great deal of effort to find and keep
_____ .

**Review the material in this section to prepare for the Self Test.** The Self Test will
check your understanding of this section and will review the other section. Any
items you miss on this test will show you what areas you will need to restudy in
order to prepare for the unit test.

# SELF TEST 2

**Write the correct answer on the blank** (4 points each answer).

**2.01**     The land in the New Territories is needed for _____ .

**2.02**     Some people do not live on land in Hong Kong, instead they live on _____ in the harbor.

**2.03**     The British forced China to trade _____ for their tea and silks.

**2.04**     The British lease of the New Territories was for _____ years.

**2.05**     Many of the people of Hong Kong came there as _____ to escape communism in China.

**2.06**     The people of Hong Kong are known for their _____ .

**2.07**     Sydney was started as a _____ colony.

**2.08**     The most important holiday in Hong Kong is _____ .

**2.09**     The government of Hong Kong was run by the _____ until 1997.

**2.010**     Sydney is _____ of the equator.

**Answer _true_ or _false_** (2 points each answer).

**2.011**     _____    Hong Kong is very spread out.

**2.012**     _____    Hong Kong was safe during World War II.

**2.013**     _____    Communist China did not want Hong Kong back.

**2.014**     _____    The water around Hong Kong is too polluted for people to make a living by fishing.

**2.015**     _____    People from Sydney are called Sydneysiders.

**2.016**     _____    Hong Kong is a duty-free port.

**2.017**     _____    Chinese people do not believe in good or bad luck.

**2.018**     _____    Chinese opera is stories of ancient China told with music and beautiful costumes.

**2.019** _____ Hong Kong cooks prefer canned or frozen food.

**2.020** _____ Sydney began to be successful as a colony when the farmers began raising pigs.

**Match each answer with the correct letter** (3 points each answer).

**2.021** _____ Victoria

**2.022** _____ Golden Gate

**2.023** _____ Confucius

**2.024** _____ Harbour Bridge

**2.025** _____ Kowloon

**2.026** _____ *feng shui* man

**2.027** _____ Bun Festival

**2.028** _____ Opera House

**2.029** _____ Buddhism

**2.030** _____ opium

a.  fortune teller

b.  most important man in Chinese history

c.  an addictive drug

d.  former capital of Hong Kong

e.  city on the peninsula across from Hong Kong Island

f.  bridge across the mouth of San Francisco Bay

g.  celebration to make ghosts happy with food

h.  roof looks like sails in the wind

i.  bridge across Port Jackson

j.  religion from India

**Answer these questions in complete sentences** (5 points each answer).

**2.031** What are some differences between Sydney and Hong Kong?

_____

_____

_____

**2.032** Why can things be bought so cheaply in Hong Kong?

_____

_____

# HISTORY & GEOGRAPHY 402

## LIFEPAC TEST

NAME _____

DATE _____

SCORE _____

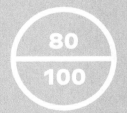

# HISTORY & GEOGRAPHY 402: LIFEPAC TEST

**Put the correct name of the seaport city on the blank** (3 points each answer).

1. _____ began as a penal colony.
2. _____ Muslim holidays are celebrated.
3. _____ is the capital of the Ottoman Empire.
4. _____ is the capital of the British Empire.
5. _____ The land was taken by the British after the Opium Wars.
6. _____ is in the Southern Hemisphere.
7. _____ Romans founded the city in A.D. 43.
8. _____ is in Asia and Europe.
9. _____ Chinese New Year is the biggest holiday.
10. _____ Many of the people are refugees from China.

**Choose the correct answer from the list** (2 points each answer).

| isthmus | archipelago | continent | ocean |
| sea | strait | mouth | island |
| peninsula | harbor | | |

11. Australia is a _____.
12. Istanbul is on the _____ of Marmara.
13. The Philippines Islands are an _____.
14. The city of Victoria is on Hong Kong _____.
15. Asia and Africa are connected by the _____ of Suez.
16. The English Channel is a _____ between England and France.

# A TRIP AROUND THE WORLD

This is the map for the geography assignment in History 402. Please pull this map out and follow the instructions that are throughout this LIFEPAC. Have fun learning about God's world!

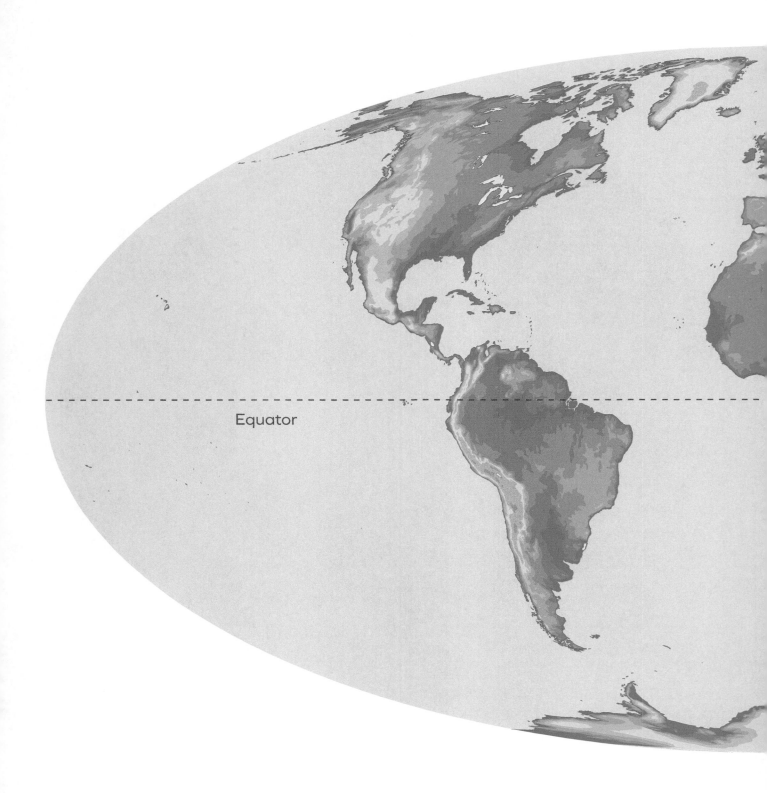

Equator

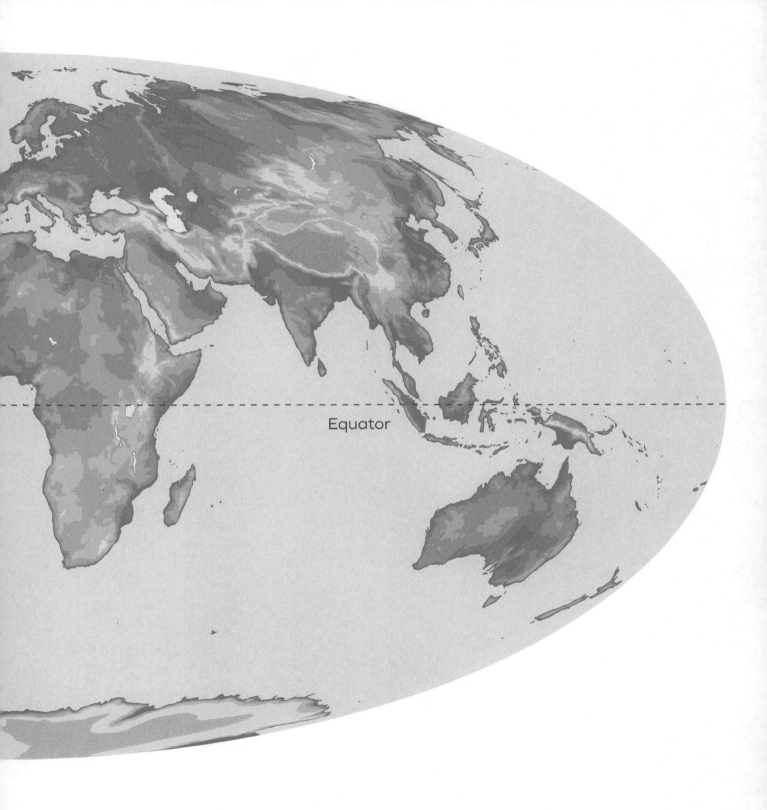

Equator

17. The Golden Gate Bridge is across the _____ of San Francisco Bay.

18. All of the cities you studied had an excellent _____ for ships.

19. San Francisco is built on a _____ between the Bay and the Pacific Ocean.

20. The Atlantic _____ is between London and the Panama Canal.

**Match these items** (2 points each answer).

21. _____ Ramadan

22. _____ Winston Churchill

23. _____ Hagia Sophia

24. _____ Buckingham Palace

25. _____ Confucius

26. _____ *feng sui* man

27. _____ Constantine

28. _____ mosque

29. _____ Opera House

30. _____ Captain James Cook

a. Chinese fortune teller

b. Muslim month of fasting

c. Sydney landmark

d. most important man in China's history

e. first Christian Roman emperor

f. explored Australia

g. British Prime Minister during World War II

h. Byzantine church

i. home of the British monarch

j. Muslim church

**Fill in the blank with the correct word** (2 points each answer).

31. Sydney became a successful colony when the farmers began raising _____ .

32. The Roman/Byzantine name for the city of Istanbul was _____ .

33. The old part of London that is now a business area is called _____ .

34. People who live in Sydney are called _____ .

35. A _____ is someone who was born within the sound of the bells of St. Mary-le-Bow in London.

36. The people of Hong Kong are famous for their _____ .

37. The British forced China to trade _____ , an addictive drug, for tea and silk.

**38.** The two parts of the British congress are the House of _____

and the House of _____ .

**39.** William the Conqueror built the White Tower, which was the first part of the

_____ , most famous as a prison.

**40.** Sydney was settled mostly by people from the country of _____ .

**Answer *true* or *false*** (1 point each answer).

**41.** _____ Hong Kong is a very crowded city.

**42.** _____ The Trooping of the Colour celebrates Australia's independence.

**43.** _____ The First Fleet brought the first Greek settlers to Byzantium.

**44.** _____ The London Blitz almost destroyed the city during World War II.

**45.** _____ The people of Sydney like outdoors activities, such as bushwalking
and yachting.

**46.** _____ The Hong Kong Bun Festival is supposed to make ghosts happy.

**47.** _____ London is the largest city in Australia.

**48.** _____ Hong Kong cooks want their food to be fresh.

**49.** _____ The Ottoman Turks attacked Europe, but were stopped at Vienna.

**50.** _____ The Golden Horn is the estuary that is the harbor for London.

**2.033**   Why do people like to visit Hong Kong?

_____

_____

_____

**Circle the correct answer** (1 point each answer).

**2.034**   When it is summer in America, it is ( fall / winter / spring ) in Sydney.

**2.035**   Decorations made of iron on houses are called Sydney

( ironwork / filigree / lace ).

**2.036**   Hong Kong is next to the South China ( Ocean / Sea / Strait ).

**2.037**   Sydney, Hong Kong, and San Francisco are all on the

( Pacific / Indian / Atlantic ) Ocean.

**2.038**   Hong Kong is in ( Europe / Australia / Asia ).

**Teacher check:**

Score _____

Initials _____

Date _____

$\dfrac{88}{110}$

# 3. ISTANBUL, WHERE EAST MEETS WEST

The ship sails from Hong Kong south along the coast of Asia, through the Indian Ocean, past India, and then north to the Gulf of Aden by the Arabian Peninsula. Then it sails into the Red Sea, where the children of Israel once crossed on dry land. The ship goes into the Gulf of Suez and through the Suez Canal. The canal is dug across the Isthmus of Suez that connects Africa to Asia. The Nile River and its delta are to the west of the ship. By using the canal, the ship sails right into the Mediterranean Sea without having to sail around Africa.

In the Mediterranean Sea, the ship sails north along the coast of Asia Minor (Turkey) and through the Aegean Sea. Heading toward the Black Sea, the ship stops in the Sea of Marmara, with Europe on one side of the ship and Asia on the other. There, where East meets West, is the city of Istanbul.

## Objectives

**Review these objectives.** When you have completed this section, you should be able to:

1. Locate on a world map the places mentioned in the text and places along the route.
2. Tell about the history of each of the seaport cities.
3. Name the places in each city that are of special interest to visitors.
4. Tell a little about how people live in each city.
5. Recognize geography terms and use them.

# Vocabulary

**Study these new words.** Learning the meanings of these words is a good study habit and will improve your understanding of this LIFEPAC.

**architect** (är′ kə tekt). A person who makes plans for buildings.

**descendant** (di sen′ dənt). A person born of a certain family. You are a descendant of your parents, grandparents, great-grandparents, and so on, back to Adam and Eve.

**dome** (dōm). A large, rounded roof.

**empire** (em′ pīr). A group of nations or states under one ruler or government.

**estuary** (es′ chü ãr ē). A part of the sea that goes inland to meet the mouth of a river.

**occupy** (ok′ yə pī). To take over another country, then put soldiers and rulers there.

**pagan** (pā′ gən). Person who worships many gods or no god.

**Pronunciation Key:** hat, āge, cãre, fär; let, ēqual, tėrm; it, īce; hot, ōpen, ôrder; oil; out; cup, put, rüle; child; long; thin; /ŦH/ for then; /zh/ for measure; /u/ or /ə/ represents /a/ in about, /e/ in taken, /i/ in pencil, /o/ in lemon, and /u/ in circus.

### Complete this map activity.

**3.1** On your world map, label the Arabian Peninsula, the Red Sea, the Isthmus of Suez, the Mediterranean Sea, Asia Minor, and the Black Sea. Mark and label Istanbul. Draw in the Nile River and its delta. Draw the ship's route from Hong Kong to Istanbul.

✔ **Teacher check:**

Initials _____      Date _____

# Ancient City

Istanbul has had many names in its long history. It began as a Greek city called Byzantium, about 700 years before Jesus was born. Eventually, it was captured by the Romans. The biggest change for the city came under the first Christian Roman emperor, Constantine. (All of the emperors before him had been **pagans**, who often killed Christians.)

In the year A.D. 330, Constantine made the town of Byzantium the new capital of the Roman **Empire** (instead of Rome). He called it New Rome, but it quickly became known as Constantinople. Although some remnants of the old city were kept, the new city that Constantine built on the site was four times larger than the original. Shortly after that, the Roman Empire was divided into two parts. The capital of the Western Empire was Rome, and the capital of the Eastern Empire was Constantinople. The Eastern Empire became known as the Byzantine Empire, after the old name of the city.

| Roman coin of Constantine

Constantinople was a strong city, and Byzantium was a strong empire. The Roman Empire in the west fell apart, and there was no strong government there for many years. However, the Byzantine Empire continued to exist for a thousand years after the western half was destroyed. The high walls around Constantinople were protection against enemies. Only twice in its history was the city captured. The first time was when men from the west came to fight against the Turks in Israel. Instead, they attacked Constantinople and captured it because they wanted the wealth of the city. The rulers of Byzantium eventually got it back. Unfortunately, the second time it was captured they could not get it back.

The second time the city was defeated, it was attacked by the Ottoman Turks. These people were warriors who were spreading the religion of Islam. They believed their God wanted them to capture the world and make everyone follow their religion. The Byzantine Empire was Christian. The Turks spent many years capturing Byzantine lands, but for a long time they could not take the city of Constantinople. The Ottoman sultan (ruler), Mehmet II, finally conquered the city in 1453.

Mehmet renamed the city Istanbul and made it the capital of *his* empire. The Ottoman Empire was very powerful. It was also very dangerous to Christian Europe. After capturing Istanbul, the Ottomans took land all along the northern coast of Africa and around the Arabian peninsula. They also pushed north into Europe, capturing Greece and parts of Hungary and Russia. The Christians of Europe were very frightened. They did not want to be ruled by these people who would destroy their country and their religion.

A very important battle took place in 1529 at the city of Vienna, Austria in Europe. The European Christians prevented the Turks from capturing the city. This stopped the Turkish advance into Europe and saved the Christian nations there. The Turks tried again later, but they were never able to go any further.

From that time on the Ottoman Empire began to *decline*, or become smaller and less powerful. As the years passed, the Turks lost wars and pieces of their land. The sultans tried to force the empire to fight and work harder. One of the ways they tried was to kill people who were not Muslims. Many Christians died very cruel deaths when the Ottomans were trying to save their empire.

The Ottoman Empire fell after World War I (1914-1918). The Ottomans fought on the German side and, therefore, lost the war. The Allies who won the war **occupied** the Ottoman Empire and made large parts of it into new, free countries. All that was left was the country we now call Turkey. The Turkish people rebelled against the sultan and set up a republic. Then they moved the capital from Istanbul to Ankara.

---

 **Put the correct answer on the blank.**

**3.2**   The city of Istanbul was at first called _____ .

**3.3**   The Eastern Roman Empire was called the _____ Empire.

**3.4**   The first Christian Roman emperor was _____ .

**3.5**   New Rome quickly became known by the name _____ .

**3.6**   The Eastern Roman Empire continued for _____ years after the Western Empire was gone.

**3.7**     The capital of the Western Roman Empire was _____ .

The capital of the Eastern Roman Empire was _____ .

**Match these items.**

**3.8** _____ Islam

**3.9** _____ Mehmet II

**3.10** _____ Ankara

**3.11** _____ Battle of Vienna (1529)

a.  renamed the city Istanbul

b.  religion of the Turks

c.  capital of Turkish Republic

d.  stopped Turks in Europe

**Answer *true* or *false*.**

**3.12** _____ The Ottoman Empire ended after World War I.

**3.13** _____ The Ottoman Empire was ruled by a sultan.

**3.14** _____ Ankara was the capital of the Ottoman Empire.

**3.15** _____ The Turks never captured any land in Europe.

**Complete the following.**

**3.16**     List the three names for the city of Istanbul and the group that gave the city that name.

a. _____ ,     _____

b. _____ ,     _____

c. _____ ,     _____

# Memories of Great Empires

Istanbul is the largest city in Turkey. It is on two peninsulas on either side of the Bosporus, the **strait** between the Sea of Marmara and the Black Sea. That means part of the city (on the eastern side) is in Asia and part (on the western side) is in Europe. Two of the longest suspension bridges in the world cross there from Asia to Europe.

The European side of the city is the part full of history. This was the old city of Constantinople and the home of the Ottoman sultans. Cutting the old city into two parts is an **estuary** called the Golden Horn (for its shape). This was the harbor for the ancient city and still is in use today. Walls ran from the coast all the way around the city, making it very difficult to attack. Much of the old wall is still standing, and a visitor can walk around it in about a day. The harbor itself was blocked by a chain that could be moved to let in friendly ships.

| The Golden Horn in Istanbul

**Answer *true* or *false*.**

**3.17** _____ The Golden Horn was blown to warn of an attack.

**3.18** _____ The harbor used to be blocked by a chain to protect the city.

**3.19** _____ Istanbul is the second largest city in Turkey.

**3.20** _____ Part of the city is in Asia and part is in Africa.

**3.21** _____ The Asian side of the city was Constantinople.

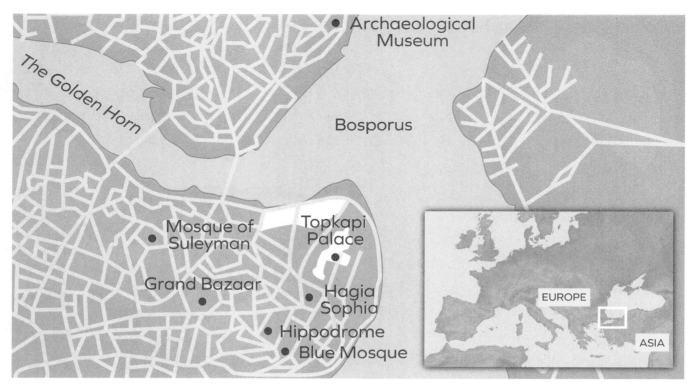

| Istanbul, where East meets West

 **Complete these map activities.**

**3.22**     Mark the mouth of the harbor with an "**X**."

**3.23**     Draw an arrow on the Bosporus showing which way a ship would go to reach the Black Sea.

**3.24**     Find and circle a peninsula.

**Teacher check:**

Initials _____

Date _____

The old city is full of buildings, parks, museums, and places that remember the great empires that ruled it. One of the most famous buildings is the Hagia Sophia. This beautiful church was first built by Constantine and later rebuilt by Justinian I, the greatest Byzantine emperor, about 1,500 years ago. It is covered by a huge **dome** and beautiful Byzantine art. The Ottomans made it into a mosque (an Islamic church), but today it is a museum. There are several other churches, now museums, that were built by the Romans and Byzantines.

With so much history, Istanbul is full of museums. There are museums of art, military history, naval history, and even carpets. One museum shows the beautiful pictures made from different colored tiles (called mosaics) that the Roman emperors used to have on the floor of their palace.

| Flag of Turkey

There are several reminders of the Romans in Istanbul. One is the Hippodrome, an ancient racetrack used for chariot races. What is left is now a park. There is also a piece of an old Roman aqueduct that is still in very good shape. Aqueducts were special pipes built on bridges to bring water into Roman cities. This one was built 1,600 years ago!

The old Roman palace is in ruins now, but you can still see some of the walls and pillars where it once stood. The palaces of the sultans, on the other hand, are still standing, and visitors can see them. The most important is the Topkapi Palace, which was the sultan's main home for many years. The palace has the sultan's ornaments, furniture, and personal items on display. They shine with gold and jewels. His throne is decorated with silk and pearls.

Just as Christians like to build beautiful churches, Muslims like to build beautiful mosques. Istanbul has many mosques built by important Ottoman sultans. Mosques cannot be decorated with pictures of real things (plants or animals), so they are decorated with beautiful designs and patterns.

The Blue Mosque gets its name from the blue windows and tiles that color everything inside it. Another mosque is named for Suleiman the Magnificent, one of the greatest of the sultans. He was the ruler who almost conquered Europe. He is buried in his mosque, which was designed by Koca Sinan, who was considered to be one of the greatest Muslim **architects** of all time.

| The Blue Mosque in Istanbul

**Put the correct answer on the blank.**

**3.25**   A Muslim church is called a _____ .

**3.26**   The sultan's main home in Istanbul was the _____ Palace.

**3.27**   An aqueduct brings _____ into the city.

**3.28**   The sultan that almost conquered Europe was _____ .

**3.29**   The Roman racetrack was called the _____ .

**3.30**   The most famous building in Istanbul is the church, _____ .

**3.31**   The greatest Byzantine emperor was _____ .

# Turkish Life

Most of the people in Istanbul are Turkish Muslims. They follow the religion of Islam. They believe in one god, but they believe they can only get to heaven if they are good enough. (This is called salvation by works.) They must follow the rules of Islam and then, maybe, god will let them into heaven when they die. Christians know that no one can be good enough to earn his own salvation (way to heaven). We trust Jesus to give us salvation when we accept Him as our Lord.

Islam has many rules that are very strict. The people of Istanbul and much of Turkey do not follow these strict rules. Women in Istanbul do not follow the strict dress codes of more fundamental Islamic nations. They dress in a more westernized fashion. They can hold jobs and vote in elections. This is not true in strict Muslim countries. The people of Istanbul also drink wine and other drinks that strict Muslims will not touch. Most Turkish people like the fact their government does not force them to follow the strict rules. There are some, however, who want the rules made into law. They often fight with the government about it.

The people of Istanbul celebrate the Muslim holidays, as we do the Christian. There is a month, called *Ramadan*, when people fast (do not eat) during the daylight hours. It ends with a three-day festival, called the Sugar Holiday, in early March. It is a time for giving gifts and eating. The most important holiday is the Festival of Sacrifice. Muslims believe that they are **descendants** of Abraham's son Ishmael. They also believe it was Ishmael, not Isaac, whom Abraham was ordered to sacrifice to God. They hold a week-long celebration in May to remember Abraham's faithfulness.

Istanbul also celebrates national Turkish holidays. Their *Cumhuriyet Bayrami* is similar to our Fourth of July. They celebrate the beginning of their republic after the sultan was forced to leave. They hold parades just like we do in America. They also have a holiday to remember the first time their Congress ever met.

No holiday would be complete without food. Turkish food is a mixture of European, Asian, and African. Do you know why that is true? Reread the history of the Ottoman Turks if you are not sure.

The most famous Turkish food is *kebabs*. These are small pieces of meat, often lamb, and vegetables put on a long skewer (thin piece of metal), then cooked over a charcoal fire. Another is *dolmas* (meaning "stuffed"), which are vegetables or grape leaves filled with seasoned meat and rice and served hot. Street merchants sell snacks and sweets. *Baklava* has thin layers of pastry and nuts soaked in honey. It is one of the better-known Turkish treats. There are even men selling sweet fruit drinks on the streets of Istanbul. They carry large silver urns on their backs. They make a fancy show of pouring a drink for a customer.

| Turkish food: kebabs and baklava

**Match these items.**

3.32 _____ *Cumhuriyet Bayrami*      a.   most famous Turkish food

3.33 _____ Ramadan      b.   son of Abraham

3.34 _____ *kebabs*      c.   Turkish Fourth of July

3.35 _____ Festival of Sacrifice      d.   month of fasting

3.36 _____ Ishmael      e.   ends time of fasting

3.37 _____ Sugar Holiday      f.   honors Abraham's faithfulness

**Complete the following sentences.**

3.38   Vegetables stuffed with meat and rice are called _____ .

3.39   Islam is a religion that believes in salvation by _____ .

3.40   Islam has many strict _____ that are not followed in Istanbul.

3.41   One of the better known Turkish sweets is _____ , made with layers of pastry and chopped nuts soaked in honey.

There are many places to shop in Istanbul. The Grand Bazaar is the largest covered marketplace in the world. There are over 4,000 shops and 67 streets there! Each street has its own special items for sale such as jewelry or brass pots. It is huge, and without a guide it is easy to get lost. The Egyptian Bazaar opened after the Ottomans conquered that country. They began bringing in Egyptian spices to sell. The bazaar is full of spices and food.

| Istanbul Grand Bazaar

Men in Turkey like to visit coffee houses. There they drink coffee or tea while they talk or play backgammon. They drink tea often. It is made very strong and sweet. Sometimes they smoke tobacco in a pipe called a hookah. The smoke in a hookah goes down into a container of water which cools it off before the man smokes it.

Another popular place to visit is a Turkish bath. The Romans always had large public baths in their cities. Istanbul continues that tradition. The baths are set up so that men go one place and women another. The bath house is kept very hot by a large fire under the floor, the same way the Romans did it. A worker at the bath house gives the customer a rubdown while he relaxes. Then, he washes up, rinses off, and leaves, fresh and clean.

Most people get around Istanbul on buses, ferries, or *dolmus*. A *dolmus* ("stuffed," like the food) is a large car that is driven around the city like a bus. It follows a certain route, but people can get on and off anywhere. These are often big American cars made in the 1950s or 60s.

There are over six and a half million people in Istanbul. They work in the city's many factories and the port, which is Turkey's busiest. Ships are built and repaired along the harbor. In many ways, Istanbul is a normal, modern city with skyscrapers and businesses. It is also a city where history is all around, and another continent is just across town.

**Answer these questions.**

**3.42**   Who started the tradition of large, heated public baths?

_____

**3.43**   How do people get around Istanbul?

_____

**3.44**   What is the world's largest covered marketplace called?

_____

**3.45**   What do men do while they drink at a coffee house?

_____

**Review the material in this section to prepare for the Self Test.** The Self Test will check your understanding of this section and will review the other sections. Any items you miss on this test will show you what areas you will need to restudy in order to prepare for the unit test.

# SELF TEST 3

**Write the correct answer on the blank** (3 points each answer).

3.01   The Greeks called Istanbul, _____ .

3.02   The capital of the Byzantine Empire was _____ .

3.03   The _____ named the city Istanbul.

3.04   Sydney is in _____ .

3.05   The Ottoman Empire fell after _____ .

3.06   The Hagia Sophia is a famous Byzantine _____ .

3.07   The largest covered marketplace in the world is the _____ .

3.08   Most of the people in Hong Kong are _____ .

3.09   To get from Sydney to San Francisco you must cross the _____ Ocean.

3.010  A ship can go from the Red Sea to the Mediterranean Sea through the _____ Canal.

**Circle the correct answer** (2 points each answer).

3.011  The Nile River is in ( Africa / Europe / South America ).

3.012  Asia Minor is ( a sea / a peninsula / an archipelago ).

3.013  Istanbul is in the ( northern / southern ) hemisphere.

3.014  Sydney became a successful colony after ( cows / sheep / farm equipment ) came there.

3.015  The Philippines is ( a river / an archipelago / a strait ).

3.016  The Coral ( Ocean / Sea / River ) is by Australia.

3.017  ( Sydney / San Francisco / Hong Kong ) is "down under" the equator.

3.018  ( Africa / Bosporus / the Arabian Peninsula ) is a continent.

3.019  Chinese people believe in ( good luck / being lazy / canned food ).

3.020  The ( South China / Marmara / Indian ) is an ocean.

**Match each answer with the correct letter** (2 points each answer).

| | | |
|---|---|---|
| **3.021** _____ First Fleet | | a. meat and vegetables on a skewer |
| **3.022** _____ sultans | | b. brings water into a city |
| **3.023** _____ Ankara | | c. month of Muslim fasting |
| **3.024** _____ Hippodrome | | d. Ottoman rulers |
| **3.025** _____ aqueduct | | e. biggest holiday in Hong Kong |
| **3.026** _____ mosque | | f. "stuffed" cars used to get around town |
| **3.027** _____ Festival of Sacrifice | | g. pipe for tobacco |
| **3.028** _____ Ramadan | | h. capital of Turkish Republic |
| **3.029** _____ kebabs | | i. Muslim church |
| **3.030** _____ hookah | | j. brought first prisoners to Sydney |
| **3.031** _____ *dolmus* | | k. Roman racetrack for chariots |
| **3.032** _____ Chinese New Year | | l. honors Abraham's faithfulness |

**Answer *true* or *false*** (1 point each answer).

**3.033** _____ Hong Kong is one of the most crowded cities in the world.

**3.034** _____ The Byzantine Empire continued for 1,000 years after the Western Roman Empire fell apart.

**3.035** _____ Suleiman the Magnificent was the first Christian Roman emperor.

**3.036** _____ The tradition of the Turkish bath was begun by the Romans.

**3.037** _____ The Opera House and Harbour Bridge are two famous landmarks in San Francisco.

**3.038** _____ The British fought two wars with China to force them to trade for opium.

**3.039** _____ Justinian I was a Byzantine emperor.

**3.040** _____ The Ottoman Empire was stopped from taking Europe at the Battle of Vienna in 1529.

**3.041** _____ The Golden Horn is the name of Hong Kong's harbor.

**3.042** _____ Hong Kong is famous for its huge parks and beaches.

**3.043** _____ Constantinople was a well-protected city, difficult to attack.

**Answer the following using complete sentences** (5 points each answer).

**3.044** Describe the religion of Hong Kong.

_____

_____

_____

_____

**3.045** Describe the religion of Istanbul.

_____

_____

_____

_____

**3.046** Where is Istanbul? Name the waterways around it.

_____

_____

_____

_____

✓ **Teacher check:**          Initials _____      80
   Score _____   Date _____      / 100

# 4. LONDON, HOME OF KINGS AND QUEENS

From Istanbul, the ship sails back out into the Mediterranean and then heads west. It passes south of the Italian Peninsula and through the Strait of Gibraltar into the Atlantic Ocean. The ship goes around the Iberian Peninsula (Spain and Portugal) and into the English Channel, the strait between France and Great Britain.

The weather is cooler now, and rain may be falling. At the mouth of the River Thames (temz) on the southeastern coast of England, the ship turns and follows the river to London. Like Istanbul, London is an ancient city, full of history.

On your world map mark the Italian Peninsula, the Iberian Peninsula, the Strait of Gibraltar, and the English Channel. Mark and label London. Draw the ship's route from Istanbul to London.

✓ **Teacher check:**

Initials _____ Date _____

# Objectives

**Review these objectives.** When you have completed this section, you should be able to:

1.  Locate on a world map the places mentioned in the text and places along the route.
2.  Tell about the history of each of the seaport cities.
3.  Name the places in each city that are of special interest to visitors.
4.  Tell a little about how people live in each city.
5.  Recognize geography terms and use them.

# Vocabulary

**Study these new words.** Learning the meanings of these words is a good study habit and will improve your understanding of this LIFEPAC.

**armor** (är′ mər). A cover worn to protect the body when fighting.

**Bubonic Plague** (byü bon′ ik  plāg). A deadly, very contagious disease, carried by fleas and rats.

**cathedral** (kə thē′ drəl). A large or important church.

**document** (dok′ yə mənt). Something written or printed that gives information which can be used to prove a fact or facts.

**Gothic** (goth′ ik). A way of making buildings look a certain way that was popular in Europe in the Middle Ages (A.D. 1200-1500). Uses high, pointed arches, tall, thin windows, and tall steeples or spires.

**memorial** (mə môr′ ē əl). Something that is a reminder of some event or person, such as a statue, an arch or pillar, a book, or a holiday.

**monarch** (mon′ ark). A king, queen, emperor, or other ruler.

**plaza** (plä′ zə). A public square in a city or town.

**regiment** (rej′ ə mənt). A large group of soldiers working together under the command of a colonel.

**subway** (sub′ wā). An underground electric railroad running beneath the surface of the streets in a city.

**traitor** (trā′ tər). A person who betrays a trust, especially his country's trust.

**tribe** (trīb). A group of people sharing the same customs, language, and ancestors, forming a community under one leader or group of leaders.

**Pronunciation Key:** hat, āge, cãre, fär; let, ēqual, tėrm; it, īce; hot, ōpen, ôrder; oil; out; cup, pùt, rüle; child; long; thin; /ŦH/ for then; /zh/ for measure; /u/ or /ə/ represents /a/ in about, /e/ in taken, /i/ in pencil, /o/ in lemon, and /u/ in circus.

# Romans to Royalty

London was a city started by the same Romans that captured Byzantium. Their empire covered much of Europe, the Middle East, and North Africa. The Romans conquered Britain just thirteen years after Jesus died on the cross. (In the year 2043 the city will be 2,000 years old. You may live to see that!)

The Romans built a fort and a bridge across the Thames. They called the new place Londinium.

The Romans ruled Britain from Londinium, and the town grew bigger. Roads went out from the city in all directions for traders and soldiers. A large stone wall was built around the city to protect it. Some of this wall is still standing. After almost 400 years, the Romans left Britain. Rome was being attacked, so they had to protect it. They never came back because the Western Roman Empire fell apart, and the Byzantine Empire never reached that far.

The town of London was an important city in England, even after the Romans left. It was controlled by a **tribe** called the Saxons. They eventually conquered England after many, many years of fighting. One of the last Saxon kings, Edward the Confessor, started a new city, the City of Westminster, a little to the west of London. He built the Palace of Westminster, which was the home of the king for almost 500 years. He also built a church which became known as Westminster Abbey.

The Saxon king was defeated in A.D. 1066 by William the Conqueror, a Frenchman. He made himself king of England. He was crowned in Westminster Abbey. All the British rulers since then have also been crowned there. Queen Elizabeth II, the ruler of Britain today, is descended from William the Conqueror and was crowned queen in Westminster Abbey in 1953.

William allowed London to set up its own government, but he built a strong tower just outside of London to remind them who was king. The White Tower was used as a place for his soldiers to stay and keep a watch on the city. It was the first section of the famous Tower of London.

| The Tower of London

**Put the correct answer on the blank.**

**4.1**    The Romans called the new town in Britain, _____ .

**4.2**    If London will be 2,000 years old in A.D. 2043, it was founded in _____ .

**4.3**    Rulers of Britain are crowned in _____ .

**4.4**    The first part of the Tower of London was a. _____ .

It was built by b. _____ .

**4.5**    After the Romans left, the _____ controlled London.

**4.6**    The United Kingdom of Great Britain is made up of four main parts in Europe.
Look up what they are in an encyclopedia, almanac, or online. List them.

a. _____

b. _____

c. _____

d. _____

In 1209 the first stone bridge was built across the Thames at London. This was the first of three bridges called London Bridge. It is the same bridge in the nursery rhyme, "London Bridge is Falling Down." About the same time, London elected its own mayor for the first time. He eventually became known as the "Lord Mayor of London." That is still his title today.

The city grew bigger on both sides of the Thames until it reached the city of Westminster. Westminster and its Abbey then became part of London.

Two great disasters struck London within a year of each other. In 1665 the Black Death struck London. The Black Death is another name for **Bubonic Plague**. This horrible disease killed about 68,000 people. The very next year, 1666, a huge fire (the Great Fire of London) started in the city and burned for five days! Most of the city was destroyed. It only stopped when the king ordered the houses ahead of it destroyed. That left the fire with nothing to burn, and it went out. Miraculously, only a few people died.

The old wooden city was rebuilt in stone, with many new, beautiful churches. The famous architect Christopher Wren designed more than fifty of the new churches for London. The most famous was St. Paul's **Cathedral**. It was the <u>fifth</u> church built in that location. The first had been destroyed by a pagan Roman emperor. The second was built by Emperor Constantine to replace it.

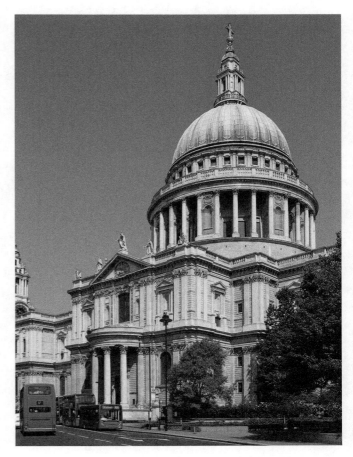

| St. Paul's Cathedral in London

By 1800 London was the largest city in the Western world. It was also the capital of a huge empire. The British built their empire with colonies all over the world. They used to say truthfully that the sun never set on the British Empire. However, most of the colonies were becoming independent around the time of World War II. The British Empire was slowly taken apart. Even today, the ruler of Great Britain is still the ruler of several countries that were once part of its empire (such as Australia).

World War II was especially difficult for London. Early in the war, the German Nazis had conquered almost all of Europe. England was the only nation fighting against them. (The United States joined the war later.) The Nazis bombed England to force them to surrender.

The London Blitz lasted from September 1940 until May 1941. The Nazis dropped bombs on the city every night! The people had to sleep in special shelters or in **subway** tunnels. Most of the city was destroyed again, and thousands of people were killed. But Britain refused to surrender! The Prime Minister (who is similar to our president), Winston Churchill, would not even consider it! He said, "We shall go on to the end ... we shall fight in the seas and oceans ... we shall fight on the beaches, ... we shall fight in the fields and in the streets, we shall fight in the hills; we shall never surrender."

After the war was won, London was rebuilt. Skyscrapers were built downtown, and it became like any modern city. Many of the old buildings, however, were repaired, so London still has its history to surround it.

**Complete these sentences.**

**4.7** The two disasters that hit London within a year of each other were:

a. _____

b. _____

**4.8** The first stone bridge built across the Thames was _____ .

**4.9** The most famous church designed by Christopher Wren was

_____ .

**4.10** London grew, and the city of _____ became part of it.

**4.11** London was the capital of the _____ Empire.

**4.12** London was almost destroyed a second time during the _____ _____ in World War II.

**4.13** _____ was the British Prime Minister who would not surrender during World War II.

**Answer these questions in complete sentences.**

**4.14** What did people mean when they said that "the sun never set on the British Empire"?

_____

_____

_____

**4.15**    Constantine built a church in London. What else did he build?

_____

_____

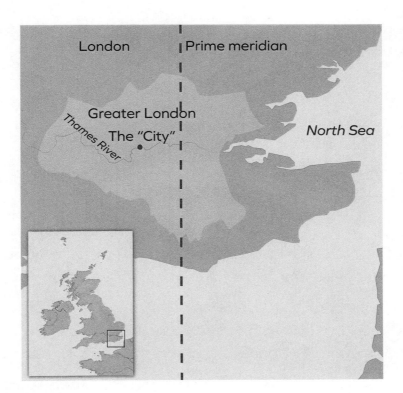

# Visiting London

London (also called Greater London) is made up of the old City of London and 32 boroughs, or towns, each with its own name and government. The "City" (spelled with a capital "C") is the area that once was inside the Roman walls. It is very small, only one square mile, while all of London is over 600 square miles. The historic places of London are usually in the City, the West End (once the city of Westminster), and the South Bank (the area right across the Thames from the City and West End). These three places are often called central London.

The Thames in London is not used as a harbor as much as it used to be. Ships used to sail right to the docks within the city (small "c" means Greater London). Today, special docks have been built closer to the ocean, away from the city. Goods are sent by truck or railroad from London to the new docks. The river in the city, therefore, is quieter and cleaner.

London has many, many fine parks. The ones in central London used to belong to the king. Now they are for everyone. The most famous are Hyde Park, Kensington Park, and Regent's Park. Kensington Palace, one of the queen's palaces, is in Kensington Park.

| Flag of Great Britain

All the way around London, in a big circle, is an area of parks called the Green Belt. This stops the city from growing any further. People must build new cities outside the Green Belt, because London stops there!

There are so many famous buildings to see in London that it is difficult to know where to start or stop. The Tower of London is one of the best to see near the City.

The first part of the Tower was built by William the Conqueror when he became king. The original White Tower has had many towers and walls added to it. It has been a prison, a fort, a place to store weapons or treasure, and a royal home over the years.

The Tower is most famous as a prison. Very rich and famous people were usually put in the Tower when they were arrested. Queen Elizabeth I spent time there as a young princess when her sister, Queen Mary, thought she was a **traitor**. She was later released. Many other nobles were killed there because they were traitors or the king thought they were. One very young king, Edward V, and his brother, disappeared in the Tower. It is believed that their uncle killed them so he could be king. The Tower has a very unhappy history.

Today the Tower is a museum. The Crown Jewels, the old, beautiful crowns and ornaments used by the king and queen, are stored there. People can come to see them. There is also a collection of old weapons and **armor**. They even have armor there for an elephant!

The Tower is guarded and cared for by men called yeomen (yō' mən) warders. The yeomen were organized in the 1400s. They are the world's oldest military group. The guards are nicknamed "Beefeaters." They act as tour guides for the Tower, as well as guards.

**Match these items.**

4.16 _____ the City

4.17 _____ White Tower

4.18 _____ Beefeaters

4.19 _____ Green Belt

4.20 _____ West End

a. circle of parks around London

b. guards at the Tower of London

c. once the city of Westminster

d. first part of the Tower of London

e. London within the old Roman walls

**Answer *true* or *false*.**

4.21 _____ The Tower is most famous as a prison.

4.22 _____ The crown jewels are kept in Westminster.

4.23 _____ Hyde and Kensington are famous London parks.

4.24 _____ Ships do not come into London very often to pick up goods.

4.25 _____ The City is very small compared to London.

4.26 _____ The Tower is still used as a prison.

---

St. Paul's Cathedral is in the City. It is the church built by Christopher Wren after The Great Fire. It is topped by a huge dome that is visible throughout the City. It took 35 years to build.

Also within the City is the Monument. This is the name for a tall pillar that is near where the fire of 1666 started. It was designed by Christopher Wren as a **memorial** of the Great Fire. It is exactly tall enough that if it is knocked over in the right direction, it will hit the spot where the fire started.

Other famous sites are in Westminster (part of the West End). This is the place where the British government is found. Westminster Palace is the home of the British Parliament (Congress). It is a huge, **gothic**-style building with rooms for both the House of Lords and the House of Commons, the two parts of the British Parliament. On top of the building's tower is a huge clock that sounds a loud bell every hour. The bell in the clock is called Big Ben.

Westminster Abbey is where rulers are crowned after they become king or queen in a huge ceremony called a coronation. Many rulers and famous people are also buried in the Abbey. People can visit and read their tombstones.

The home of the British Prime Minister is just up the road from the Parliament. The home is named simply for its address, "Number 10, Downing Street." Many of the government offices are around there on Downing Street and Whitehall, which goes from the Parliament to Trafalgar Square.

| Buckingham Palace

Trafalgar Square is a large **plaza** which honors a great British hero. His name was Admiral Nelson, and he defeated the French navy in the Battle of Trafalgar. Nelson died in the battle. A large pillar in the square has his statue on top.

The queen's London home is also near the Parliament. It is called Buckingham Palace. It is one of several palaces the royal family still owns. Another is St. James Palace, which is right across the park. People can visit Buckingham Palace and see some of the rooms during the summer, when the queen is on her vacation. (She vacations at another home in Scotland each year.)

There are also many fine museums in London. The British Museum is one of the most famous. It has many fine statues, vases, and pieces of pottery from the ancient Greeks and Romans. These were collected by the British during the time of their empire. The nearby British Library has the *Magna Carta*, the Great Charter, a famous **document** in British history. It also has a copy of the first book ever made on a movable-type printing press, a Gutenberg Bible.

There still is a London Bridge across the Thames. The first one was built in 1209 and replaced in 1831. That second bridge was sold to a businessman in the United States when it was replaced with a new one in 1973. The American took the old bridge apart, moved it to Lake Havasu, Arizona, and rebuilt it. You can see it there today.

**Complete these items.**

**4.27** St. Paul's Cathedral is topped by a huge _____ .

**4.28** The British government is located in the _____ part of London.

**4.29** Trafalgar Square honors the British hero, _____ .

**4.30** The queen's London home is _____ .

**4.31** One of the most famous museums in London is the _____ .

**4.32** The Monument is a memorial of the _____ .

**4.33** The Prime Minister lives at _____ .

**4.34** Two important things that can be found at the British Library are:

a. _____

b. _____

**4.35** The clock in the Parliament building is called _____ .

**4.36** The two parts of the British Parliament are:

a. _____

b. _____

# British Life

London is the home of the monarch of Great Britain. Since 1952, Queen Elizabeth II has been the queen. Her heir, the person who will take the throne after her, is her son, Prince Charles. Prince Charles is the Prince of Wales. Prince Charles married Lady Diana Spencer in July of 1981. Their marriage was dissolved in August of 1996, and a year later the Princess of Wales was killed in a car crash in Paris. Their two children, Prince William and Prince Harry, are second and third in line of succession to the throne.

Queen Elizabeth II has three other adult children and six grandchildren. The queen's husband is Prince Philip. He is not the King of Great Britain because Elizabeth is the nation's ruler.

London is a city that has many old ceremonies that are part of being the home of the government and the British royalty. The coronation of a new ruler always takes place in London, but this happens only when a king or queen dies and a new ruler is needed. Other ceremonies occur more often.

Every year the opening of Parliament is a special event. The queen rides to Westminster Palace in a gold-trimmed

| Changing of the Guards

coach pulled by horses. She is surrounded by mounted guards in beautiful uniforms. At the Parliament building, she puts on her royal robes and the Imperial State Crown (this is the only time during the year that she wears it). She marches into the House of Lords and sits on a throne there. The Lords are all dressed in robes and coronets (small crowns). A special officer is sent to bring in the members of the House of Commons. (He must knock three times before they let him in. Not answering right away shows that the Commons are independent of the ruler.) Then the queen reads a speech written by the Prime Minister which tells what the government hopes to do that year.

Another ceremony is the Trooping of the Colour (British spelling). This is a parade honoring the queen's official birthday. That is not the day she was born, but the day she was crowned as queen. The Colour is the name for the flag of a **regiment**. The Trooping of the Colour is actually a military parade with many grand, old uniforms. The queen herself rides in the parade.

Other ceremonies occur every day as they have for many years. The Changing of the Guard at Buckingham Palace, St. James Palace, and the Tower of London happens before noon every day (except in the winter, when it is every other day). The guards who have been on duty march out to music and are replaced by the new guards, who take their turn. It is all very exciting and colorful. The guards are dressed in red coats and tall, furry black hats.

**Match these items.**

| | | | |
|---|---|---|---|
| **4.37** | _____ monarch | a. | everyday ceremony |
| **4.38** | _____ Prince of Wales | b. | heir to the throne |
| **4.39** | _____ Trooping of the Colour | c. | Queen Elizabeth II |
| **4.40** | _____ coronation | d. | Queen's official birthday |
| **4.41** | _____ Changing of the Guard | e. | crowning a new ruler |

**Answer these questions in complete sentences.**

**4.42** Why must the officer knock three times when he summons the House of Commons to the opening of Parliament?

_____

_____

_____

**4.43** What is a Colour?

_____

_____

Inside the City is a church called St. Mary-le-Bow. Any person who is born within the sound of that church's bell is called a Cockney. These are the true Londoners. They have an accent, a way of speaking, that is all their own. It does not sound like other English speech. It is difficult for people to understand if they are not used to it. Cockney speech is less common since television and public education became common. People tend to watch television and talk the way the actors do, which is not Cockney. The teachers at school also teach standard English.

The City itself is now a business area of London. Only about 5,000 people actually live there. During the day, however, 500,000 people work there. The Bank of England, the national bank, has its main office in the City. The Bank of England is one of the most important banks in the world. It is in a very old building which is called "The Old Lady of Threadneedle Street." Many of the street names show what business used to be there. There is Milk Street, Bread Street, Honey Lane, and even a Friday Street. Friday Street sold fish at a time when the Catholic religion required people to eat fish on Friday.

| London underground (subway)

People in the boroughs near the center of London usually live in rented apartments or houses. People living further away usually live in their own houses with their own gardens. British people love to have gardens around their homes, no matter how small.

London has one of the largest subway systems in the world. There are many, many miles of track underground for people to use to get around the city. Londoners call it the "tube." There are also buses and trains to carry people to and from work or shopping. Some people do drive their own cars, but most use the public transportation.

Police officers in London are called "bobbies." They wear helmets and dark suits. Lawyers in England are called *barristers*. They wear black robes and white wigs when they go to court.

**Match these items.**

4.44 _____ bobbies

4.45 _____ Cockney

4.46 _____ the City

4.47 _____ Bank of England

4.48 _____ Friday Street

4.49 _____ the tube

4.50 _____ barristers

a. Old Lady of Threadneedle Street

b. fish were sold there

c. business area of London

d. subway, one of world's largest

e. born within the sound of the bells of St. Mary-le-Bow

f. lawyers in robes and wigs

g. London policemen

Many people in London and in Sydney, Australia belong to the Anglican Church. It is called the Church of England. The queen is the head of the church. It was the church in America when it was a British colony. The Constitution of the United States does not allow government churches like this now.

The people of London are very fond of tea. In fact, they have a small meal they call "afternoon tea." It is tea drunk with things like cake, sandwiches, and cookies. We would call it a very fancy snack. A proper tea uses china and silver to serve the food.

Soccer, which is called football in Europe, is the most popular sport in London. Rugby and cricket came from England and are still popular there. A cricket match usually lasts all day, and could last for several days! It is a very relaxed game for the people who watch. They often bring food and have a picnic while they watch.

London is Great Britain's largest city. Almost 7 million people live there. Many of them work in factories all over the city. Certain areas of London are known for a special type of factory. For example, the borough of Whitechapel is where a great deal of clothing is made. London is also still a major trading center, even if the port itself is outside the city limits.

More people visit London each year than live there! That really is not so surprising, because there is so much to see and do. London is an old city that still has plenty of life left in it.

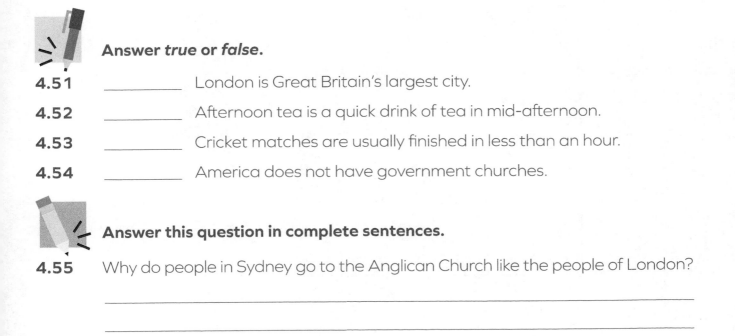

**Answer *true* or *false*.**

**4.51** _____ London is Great Britain's largest city.

**4.52** _____ Afternoon tea is a quick drink of tea in mid-afternoon.

**4.53** _____ Cricket matches are usually finished in less than an hour.

**4.54** _____ America does not have government churches.

**Answer this question in complete sentences.**

**4.55** Why do people in Sydney go to the Anglican Church like the people of London?

_____

_____

**Write the names that match these descriptions, then find the names in the puzzle** (words may be hidden down, across, or diagonally).

**4.56**   The bell in the clock on a tower of the Parliament Building _____

**4.57**   The part of London where Parliament meets _____

**4.58**   Old London is called the _____ .

**4.59**   Britain's congress is called a _____ .

**4.60**   The architect who planned St. Paul's Cathedral _____

**4.61**   The people who started London _____

**4.62**   The name used for Westminster's church _____

**4.63**   The river on which London is located _____

**4.64**   The king who built the Tower of London _____

**4.65**   The London palace for the queen _____

**4.66**   "The Old Lady of Threadneedle Street" is really a _____ .

| D | X | Q | Y | R | O | Z | E | C | T | P |
|---|---|---|---|---|---|---|---|---|---|---|
| O | W | H | E | O | R | A | V | I | O | A |
| W | E | S | T | M | I | N | S | T | E | R |
| N | R | N | B | A | B | B | E | Y | X | L |
| I | C | E | D | N | E | B | F | G | I | I |
| N | H | I | N | S | J | A | K | L | Y | A |
| G | B | U | C | K | I | N | G | H | A | M |
| M | N | O | P | Q | R | K | S | T | O | E |
| U | V | W | Z | A | B | I | G | B | E | N |
| W | I | L | L | I | A | M | Y | X | T | T |
| A | B | C | D | E | T | H | A | M | E | S |

# Back to the United States

It is time for your ship to head back to San Francisco. It sails out of London into the English Channel and out into the vast Atlantic Ocean. Traveling west, the ship goes past the Caribbean Islands to the Isthmus of Panama. There it crosses into the Pacific Ocean through the Panama Canal. Sailing north along the west coast of North America, the ship goes by the Baja Peninsula and reaches home in San Francisco Bay. Your long, eventful trip is finally finished.

**On your map mark the Caribbean Islands, the Isthmus of Panama, and the Baja Peninsula. Draw the ship's route from London to San Francisco.**

**Teacher check:**

Initials _____    Date _____

**Before you take this last Self Test, you may want to do one or more of these self checks.**

1. _____ Read the objectives. See if you can do them.
2. _____ Restudy the material related to any objectives that you cannot do.
3. _____ Use the **SQ3R** study procedure to review the material:
   a. **S**can the sections.
   b. **Q**uestion yourself.
   c. **R**ead to answer your questions.
   d. **R**ecite the answers to yourself.
   e. **R**eview areas you did not understand.
4. _____ Review all vocabulary, activities, and Self Tests, writing a correct answer for every wrong answer.

# SELF TEST 4

**Write the correct answer from the list on each blank** (3 points each answer).

| | | |
|---|---|---|
| Hong Kong | the City | Tower of London |
| Great Fire | Romans | London Bridge |
| London Blitz | British Empire | Sydney |

**4.01** The old part of London is called _____ .

**4.02** _____ is a museum that was a prison.

**4.03** Chinese refugees fled to _____ .

**4.04** London was started by the _____ .

**4.05** The first stone bridge across the Thames was _____ to escape communism in China.

**4.06** Prisoners from Great Britain were sent to the penal colony in _____ .

**4.07** _____ destroyed most of London in 1666.

**4.08** The sun never set on the _____ .

**4.09** _____ destroyed most of London during World War II.

**Match each answer with the correct letter** (3 points each answer).

**4.010** _____ Captain James Cook

**4.011** _____ Victoria

**4.012** _____ Winston Churchill

**4.013** _____ Golden Gate Bridge

**4.014** _____ Opera House

**4.015** _____ Hagia Sophia

**4.016** _____ Ramadan

**4.017** _____ Admiral Nelson

a. British prime minister during World War II

b. British hero at Trafalgar

c. building with a sail-like roof at the entrance to a harbor

d. Byzantine church

e. spans the entrance to San Francisco

f. Moslem's month of fasting

g. city on Hong Kong Island

h. explored Australia

**Answer *true* or *false*** (2 points each answer).

4.018 _____ British monarchs are crowned at Westminster Abbey.

4.019 _____ Istanbul was settled by the British.

4.020 _____ A Cockney must be born within the sound of the bells of St. Mary-le-Bow.

4.021 _____ St. Paul's Cathedral was planned by Sir Christopher Wren.

4.022 _____ Queen Elizabeth is sometimes called the "Old Lady of Threadneedle Street."

4.023 _____ The Trooping of the Colour celebrates the independence of London from the Turks.

4.024 _____ Sampans are decorated houses in Sydney.

4.025 _____ Buckingham Palace is a hotel for tourists.

4.026 _____ The Parliament building is in Westminster.

4.027 _____ The Ottoman Empire conquered all of Europe.

4.028 _____ Sydney celebrates Christmas in summer.

4.029 _____ Goods from other countries are sold cheaply in Hong Kong because they are not taxed.

**Complete these sentences with the name of a city** (3 points each answer).

4.030 The home of the British monarch is _____ .

4.031 Kowloon and the New Territories are part of _____ .

4.032 A city in the Southern Hemisphere is _____ .

4.033 The House of Commons meets in _____ .

4.034 Constantinople became _____ .

**Answer these questions in complete sentences** (5 points each answer).

**4.035**   How are Sydney and Hong Kong different?

_____

_____

_____

**4.036**   How are Istanbul and London alike?

_____

_____

_____

---

**Teacher check:**      Initials _____    **80**

Score _____     Date _____    **100**

---

**Before you take the LIFEPAC Test, you may want to do one or more of these self checks.**

1. _____ Read the objectives. See if you can do them.
2. _____ Restudy the material related to any objectives that you cannot do.
3. _____ Use the **SQ3R** study procedure to review the material.
4. _____ Review activities, Self Tests, and LIFEPAC vocabulary words.
5. _____ Restudy areas of weakness indicated by the last Self Test.